Published in 2014 by The Rosen Publishing Group, Inc.
29 East 21st Street, New York, NY 10010

Adaptations to North American Edition © 2014 by The Rosen Publishing Group, Inc.
Copyright © 2014 Axis Books Limited

First Edition

US Editor: Joshua Shadowens

Library of Congress Cataloging-in-Publication Data

Bolitho, Mark.
 Fold your own origami air force / by Mark Bolitho. — First edition.
     pages cm. — (Origami army)
 Includes index.
 ISBN 978-1-4777-1319-8 (library binding) — ISBN 978-1-4777-1469-0 (paperback) —
 ISBN 978-1-4777-1470-6 (6-pack)
 1. Origami—Juvenile literature. 2. Military miniatures—Juvenile literature. 3. Air forces—Miscellanea—Juvenile literature. I. Title.
 TT872.5.B64 2014
 736'.982—dc23
                                 2013005113

Manufactured in the United States of America

CPSIA Compliance Information: Batch #S13PK8: For Further Information contact Rosen Publishing, New York, New York at 1-800-237-9932

Fold Your Own ORIGAMI
AIR FORCE

Mark Bolitho

PowerKiDS
press.

New York

CONTENTS

INTRODUCTION

Have you ever heard of **origami**? Origami is the traditional Japanese art of folding paper to make small **sculptures** or models. It gets its name from the Japanese language. The word *ori* means "folding," and the word *kami* means "paper." Using just a single sheet of paper and some folding and creasing you can make an air force cap, a jet fighter, or even a stealth fighter!

The United States Air Force is one of the five branches of the United States Armed Forces. The air force was formed as a separate branch of the **military** in 1947 and is the youngest branch of the US military. The air force uses its planes to maintain the peace and security of the United States. The US has the world's largest air force, with over 300,000 active **personnel** and almost 6,000 aircraft as of 2012.

There are many different jobs and skills needed by people serving in the air force. The air force not only protects the sky over our heads, but also can be called upon to keep the peace in other countries, to deliver **cargo** to countries in need, and to carry out many other duties.

In this book you will find step-by-step **instructions** for making a variety of origami models that relate to the air force. You will begin by learning the basic **techniques** you will need to be successful with your projects. All you have to do is get folding and creasing, and soon you'll have your own origami air force!

MATERIALS AND EQUIPMENT

All the projects in this book are made from square or rectangular pieces of paper. Here are the basic **tools** you need, and instructions for getting your paper to the right **proportions**.

All you really need is a pair of hands and a piece of paper. To achieve the best results keeps your hands clean, and use your fingers to manipulate the paper: enhance the creases using fingertips and nails.

CHOPSTICKS
A chopstick can be very useful for manipulating the inside of a model, particularly to work on the detail and create points.

RULER
You can use different tools to help you fold and to make sure your proportions are accurate. You can use a ruler to create straight folds and to sharpen creases.

SCISSORS
A good, sharp pair of scissors is invaluable for cutting paper. The best for the task have long, straight cutting blades.

MAKING A SQUARE FROM A RECTANGLE

Always start with a true rectangle—all four corners must be 90 degrees.

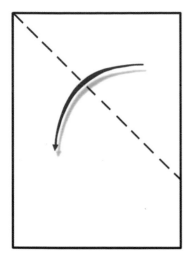

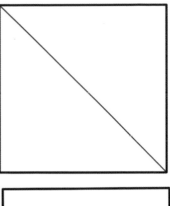

1 Fold the top edge of the paper diagonally so that the top edge aligns with the left-hand edge.

2 Fold the bottom edge of the paper up to the base of the triangle you have just made. Cut along this folded edge.

3 Unfold the triangle and the square is ready for use. You will have a square and a residual rectangle of paper.

MAKING A RECTANGLE FROM A SQUARE

Origami rectangles need to be of "A" proportions—A4, A3, A2. These stages show you how to get a rectangle of the correct proportions very simply from a sheet of square paper.

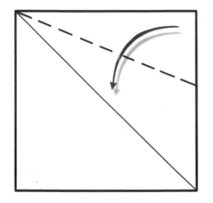

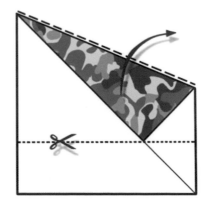

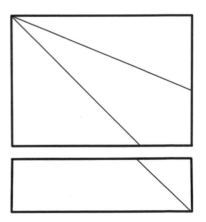

1 Fold the square in half diagonally and unfold. Now fold the top edge of your square so that it aligns with the diagonal crease.

2 Fold the lower edge of the paper up to the point at which the corner touches the diagonal crease. Cut along this crease.

3 Unfold the paper and a rectangle of the "A" proportions is ready for use. You will also have a residual rectangle.

9

BASIC TECHNIQUES

Although folding paper might seem the easiest of crafts, there are a few basic techniques to master before you can start. The construction process for each of the models in this book is illustrated using step diagrams. Alongside the diagrams you will find arrows and fold lines that show how a particular fold should be carried out. These are all explained on the following pages.

SYMBOLS

THE SYMBOLS USED IN THIS BOOK ARE BASED ON STANDARD ORIGAMI NOTATION

Fold

Fold and unfold

(2) Fold over two layers

The next step will show the model turned over

Repeat steps

(4–8) Repeat steps 4 to 8

Repeat behind

x 3 Repeat three times

Inflate the model

Squash or sink the paper inside itself

Viewpoint

X-ray view

90° Rotate the model 90 degrees

Cut

Hold the model here

BASIC FOLDS

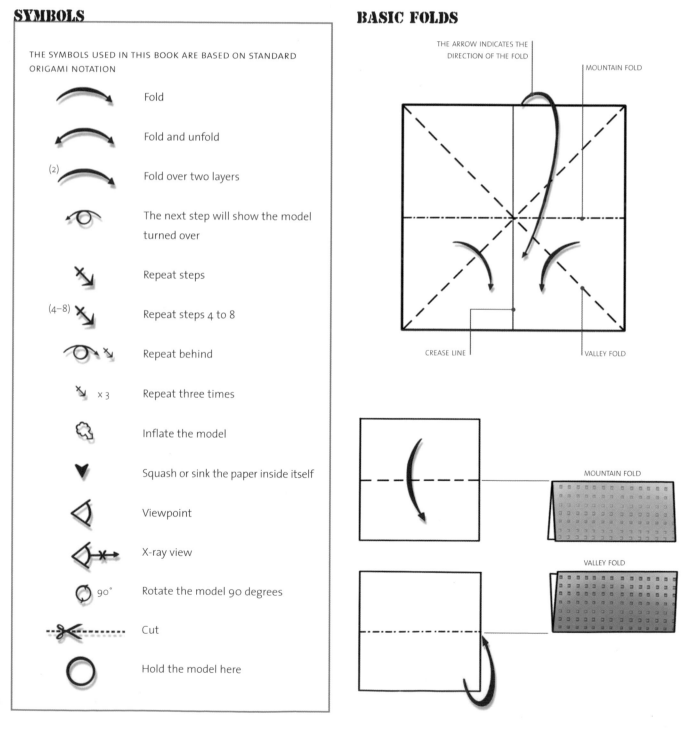

THE ARROW INDICATES THE DIRECTION OF THE FOLD

MOUNTAIN FOLD

CREASE LINE

VALLEY FOLD

MOUNTAIN FOLD

VALLEY FOLD

FOLLOWING INSTRUCTIONS

The projects are broken down into a series of simple steps. Each step has a corresponding diagram that shows you how to make that step's folds.

Before attempting a step make sure that the model you have resembles the step diagram. Each diagram shows where to make each fold. The red arrows show the direction of the fold.

When you have completed a step, carefully look at the model to see if it resembles the next step. If your model does not look right, don't worry, just look closely at the instructions and try working back until you can match your model with an earlier step.

FOLDING TIPS

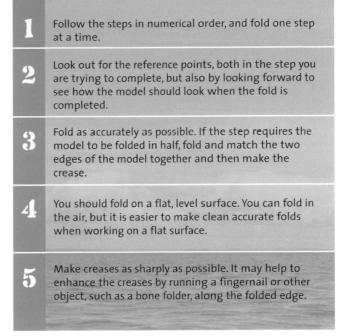

1 Follow the steps in numerical order, and fold one step at a time.

2 Look out for the reference points, both in the step you are trying to complete, but also by looking forward to see how the model should look when the fold is completed.

3 Fold as accurately as possible. If the step requires the model to be folded in half, fold and match the two edges of the model together and then make the crease.

4 You should fold on a flat, level surface. You can fold in the air, but it is easier to make clean accurate folds when working on a flat surface.

5 Make creases as sharply as possible. It may help to enhance the creases by running a fingernail or other object, such as a bone folder, along the folded edge.

FOLDING IN HALF

1 This diagram indicates that the square of paper should be folded in half.

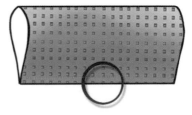

2 First of all line up the opposite edges and hold them together.

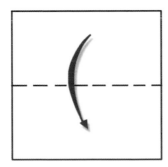

3 Now pinch at the center of the folded edge and make the crease, smoothing from the center out to the edges.

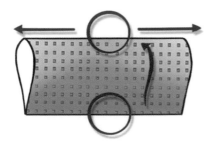

4 Keep holding the edges together as you sharpen the crease, the paper is now folded in half.

11

BASIC TECHNIQUES CONTINUED

REVERSE FOLD

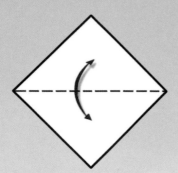

1 Fold and unfold the square of paper diagonally.

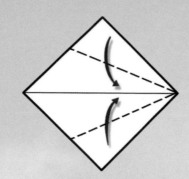

2 Fold the edges to the middle crease of the paper as shown.

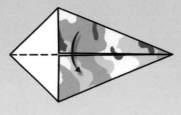

3 Fold the model horizontally, along the middle.

4 This arrow indicates a reverse fold, along the dotted line.

5 This interim stage shows the point reversing into itself.

6 The reverse fold is now complete.

PRELIMINARY BASE

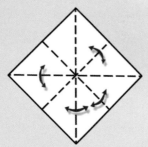

1 Fold and unfold the square in half horizontally, vertically, and diagonally.

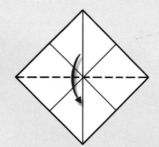

2 Fold the square in half along one of the diagonal creases.

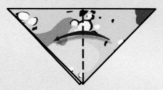

3 Fold in half again, along the center fold.

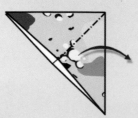

4 Slip a finger inside the top layer and lift the paper.

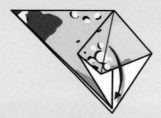

5 Squash the paper down to flatten the point.

6 Turn over and repeat steps 3 to 5. The preliminary base.

WATERBOMB BASE

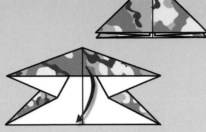

1. Fold and unfold the square in half horizontally, vertically, and diagonally.

2. Fold the square in half horizontally and reverse the folds in the diagonal creases.

3. Continue to fold and flatten the model, and it is complete.

BIRD BASE

Start with the completed preliminary base on page 12.

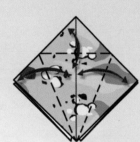

1. Fold and unfold the side edges and top corner, as shown.

2. Lift up the front layer and fold along the top crease. Fold in each of the sides.

3. Turn over and repeat steps 1 and 2 on the other side. The bird base is now complete.

FROG BASE

Start with the preliminary base on page 12.

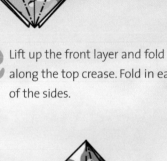

1. Fold and unfold the side edge to the center crease.

2. Open the corner and flatten the paper along the new fold.

3. Fold and unfold the lower edges to the center crease.

4. Push the center section up and back. Refold the lower edges.

5. Repeat steps 1 to 4 on the other three points.

6. The frog base is complete and should look like this.

13

AIRPLANE

A truly top-flight airplane model. It is a little more complex than the basic paper dart, but the extra steps are well worth the effort.

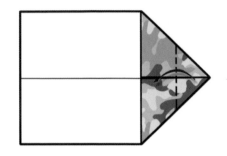

1 Start with a rectangle of paper, pattern-side down. Fold in half horizontally and unfold.

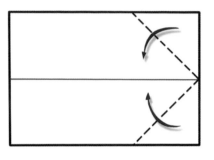

2 Fold each of the right-hand corners to the center crease.

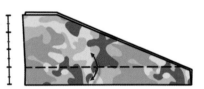

3 Now fold the pointed end in along the center crease to the point, where the patterned section ends.

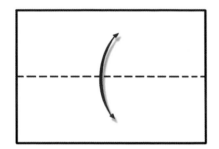

4 Fold both the edges of the paper in so that they align with the center crease.

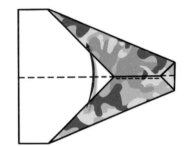

5 As neatly as possible, fold the model in half along the original center crease.

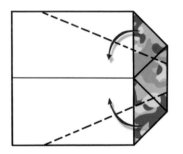

6 Fold and unfold three-quarters of each wing, parallel to the base of the model.

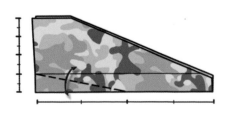

7 Fold and unfold between the fold made in step 6 and halfway along the base, as shown.

8 Reverse the fold made in step 7, making a reverse fold between the wings.

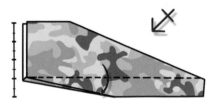

9 Now fold each wing down along the crease you made in step 6.

10 Finish the airplane by folding up the outside edge of each wing, as shown.

BOMBER

The bomber is a bit more complex than the airplane on the previous pages, but it flies brilliantly with the extra folds.

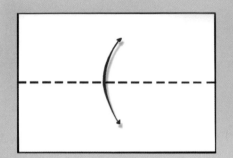

1 Start with a rectangle of paper, pattern-side down. Fold in half horizontally and unfold.

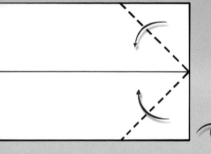

2 Fold each of the right-hand corners to the center crease. Turn the paper over.

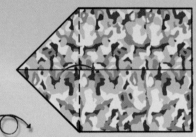

3 Now fold the point in along the center crease, to make the paper square.

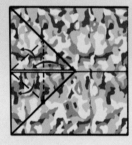

4 Fold the point back toward the edge, squashing it open as you do so.

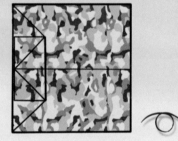

5 This is what you should have. Make sure the creases are very sharp. Turn the paper over.

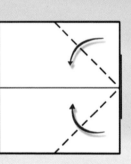

6 Fold the corners in to touch the center crease line.

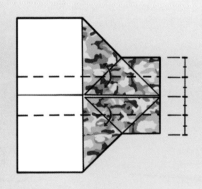

7 Fold and unfold three-quarters of each wing, parallel to the base of the model.

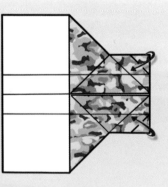

8 Fold the outermost corners in along the folds made in step 7, as shown.

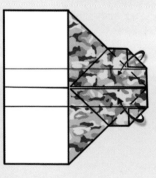

9 Fold the edges of the forward section again, to the center crease, as shown.

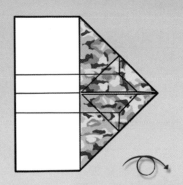

10 This is what you should have. Turn the model over.

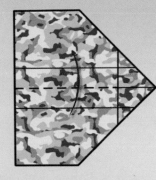

11 Fold the model in half, along the original center crease.

12 Fold each wing down along the creases made in step 7.

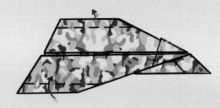

13 Finish the bomber by folding up the outside edge of each wing, as shown.

LONG-RANGE BOMBER

The success of this long-range bomber model relies on accurate folding and very sharp creases from the start.

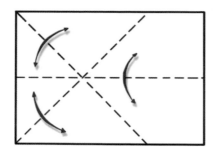 **1** Pattern-side down, fold and unfold a rectangle horizontally and then diagonally at one end.

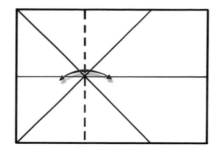 **2** Now fold and unfold the short end, creasing where the diagonals lines meet.

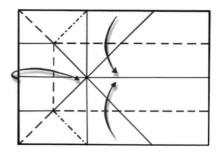 **3** Fold the long edges in to the center, and the front edge to the crease made in step 2. Turn the model over.

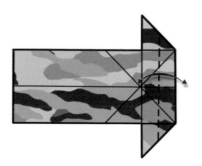 **4** Flip your model over—you should have this. Fold and unfold the right edge, as shown.

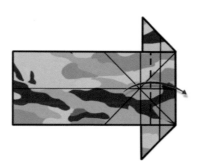 **5** Fold the left-hand (tail) edge as shown. This will cause the lower layer to open out slightly.

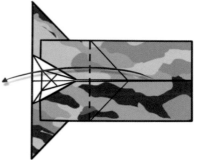 **6** Now carefully fold the tail end back to the left, using the diagonal creases as a guide.

 **7** Fold the outer edges into the center. Flatten the lower layer as it opens, and crease the folds.

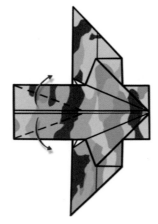 **8** Fold back the top edges of the tail out, one side at a time.

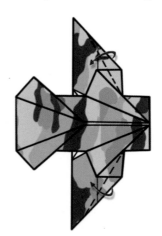 **9** Fold over the edges of the wings, then turn the model over.

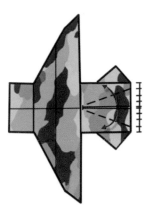

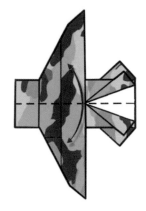

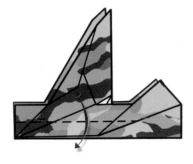

10 Fold the remaining edges of the tail out as shown.

11 Carefully fold your entire aircraft in half horizontally.

12 Now fold and unfold the front layer in half horizontally, as shown.

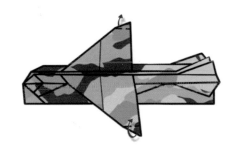

13 Use this new crease to make the nose: fold the top corner to the front, and the bottom corner to the rear.

14 Fold the wing perpendicular to the body. Repeat steps 12 to 14 on the other side.

15 Fold up the tip of each wing, and the bomber is complete.

JET FIGHTER

This jet fighter is relatively easy to make. It makes a neat little aircraft, especially when you have a whole squadron of them.

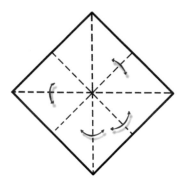

1 Pattern-side down, fold and unfold a square in half vertically, horizontally, and diagonally.

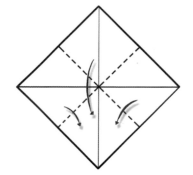

2 Fold the square in half diagonally and reverse the remaining diagonal folds.

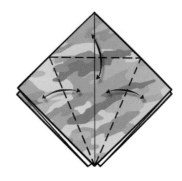

3 Fold and unfold the edges into the center, as shown.

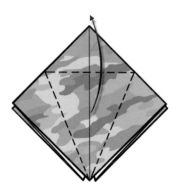

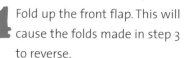

4 Fold up the front flap. This will cause the folds made in step 3 to reverse.

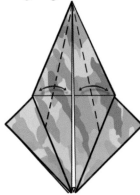

5 Fold and unfold the top edges into the center, as shown.

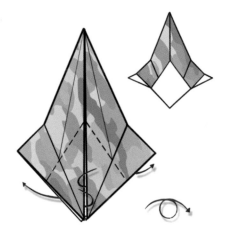

6 Grasp each bottom flap in turn. Twist each back toward the outer edge. Turn your model.

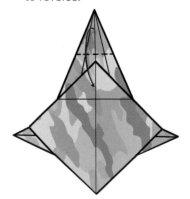

7 Fold the top point down toward the center of the model, to where the creases cross.

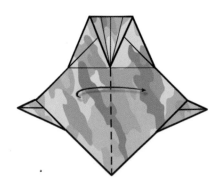

8 Taking care to be as accurate as possible, fold the model in half vertically, as shown.

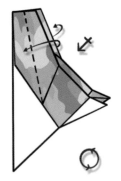

9 Fold the outer edges in half vertically on both sides. Rotate your model 90 degrees counterclockwise.

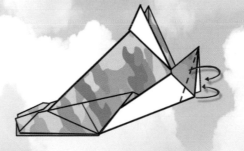

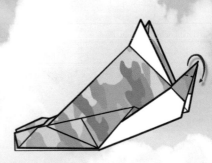

10 Fold the tail end in half along the short edge and reverse the fold into the body.

11 Fold the outer edges of the tail into the model.

12 Now reverse-fold the tip of the tail of the airplane.

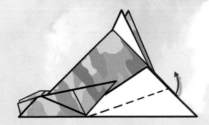

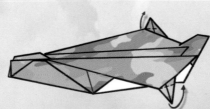

13 Fold each wing perpendicular to the body.

14 Fold up the tip of each wing. The jet fighter is complete.

STEALTH FIGHTER

The first paper airplane to use stealth technology, the iconic F-117 Nighthawk will fly undetected over your enemies airspace.

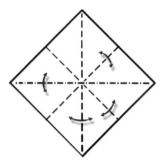

1 Fold and unfold the square in half vertically, horizontally, and diagonally, as shown.

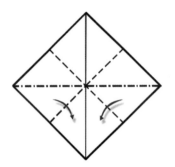

2 Fold the square in half along one diagonal crease. Reverse the remaining diagonal folds.

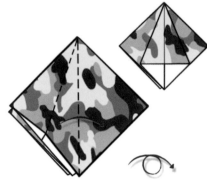

3 Fold up the front layer and squash, then turn over.

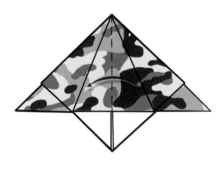

4 Fold over and open out the top layer.

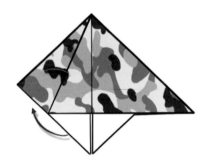

5 Reverse-fold out the corner beneath the front layer.

6 The model should look like this, now turn over.

7 Fold over one side of the front layer.

8 Fold up the front corner of the model.

9 Fold the corner back again as indicated.

10 Fold the corner back causing the edge top to fold over.

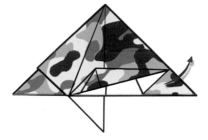

11 Carefully fold out the trapped paper on the right side.

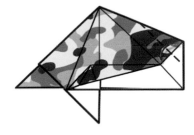

12 Fold over the edge indicated by the dotted line.

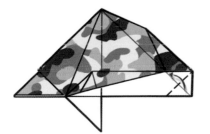

13 Fold the bottom right hand corner in.

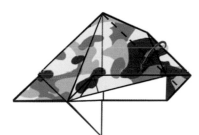

14 Fold the right edge along the line shown.

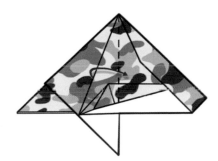

15 Now fold the front layer back over.

16 Fold over the corner to meet the center line.

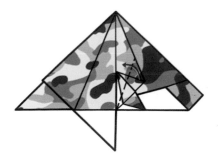

17 Fold the corner over again to meet the center line.

(7 to 18)

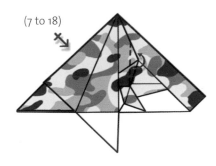

18 Fold over the edge and repeat steps 7 to 18 on the other side.

STEALTH FIGHTER CONTINUED

19 The model should look like this, turn it over.

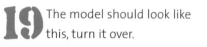

20 Fold the lower edge into the model.

21 Fold over the front layer opening the model.

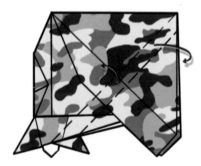

22 Fold the front layer up and down again.

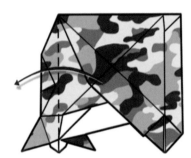

23 Now fold both of the layers back over.

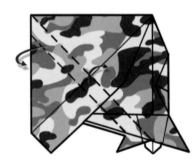

24 Fold the top layer up and down.

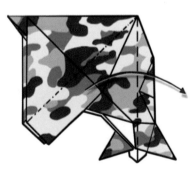

25 Fold the front layer over, holding the lower layer down and flatten the model.

26 The plane should look like this, now turn over.

27 Fold the body in half and shape the plane. The stealth fighter is now complete.

CARGO

Here is a cargo container for weapons and essential food supplies. This is origami army made easy.

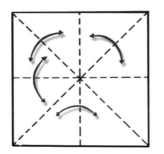

1 Pattern-side down, fold and unfold a square in half vertically, horizontally, and diagonally.

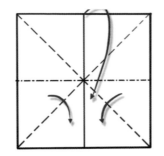

2 Fold the square in half horizontally and reverse the two diagonal folds.

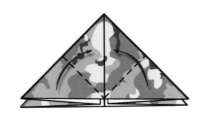

3 Fold each of the bottom corners of the top layer up to touch the top point.

4 Now as neatly as possible, fold and unfold the points in half.

5 Fold the corners at either side in to the center, making sure that the folds are vertical.

6 Fold the top corners into the folded corners from step 5, as shown.

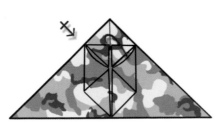

7 Tuck each of the two folded corners into the pockets of the folded edges, as shown.

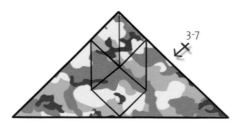

8 Turn the model over and repeat steps 3 to 7 on the reverse.

9 Fold and unfold the top and bottom corners to the center, as shown.

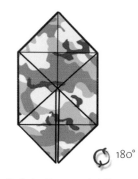

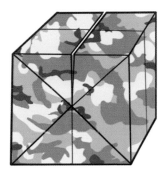

180°

10 Rotate the model through 180 degrees.

11 Blow gently into the hole to inflate the model and crease the edges to shape into a cube.

12 The cargo container is complete and ready for use.

AIR FORCE CAP

This US Air Force flight cap will have your men standing at attention! It is a simple model with straight sides and a dipped crown.

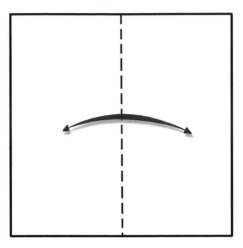

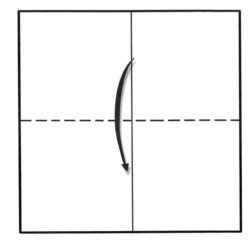

1 Start with a square of paper, pattern-side down. Fold the paper in half vertically, make a sharp crease, and unfold the paper.

2 Now fold the square of paper in half horizontally and make a sharp crease. Leave the paper folded, with the creased fold at the top.

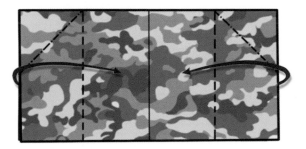

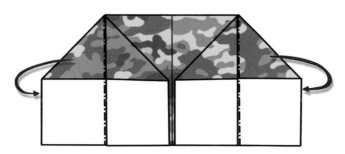

3 Fold each outside edge to the center. Make sharp creases and unfold. Now fold the right hand edge to the center crease. Repeat on the left.

4 Open each top corner out and squash flat to achieve the above illustration. Now fold each of the outer edges behind.

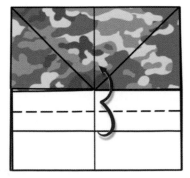

5 You should have a small square, as above. Fold the lower edge in half horizontally, so that it meets the edge of the patterned section.

6 Fold the lower edge in half again, and then fold the lower section over the colored part.

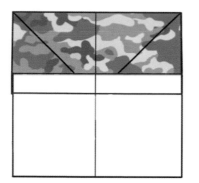

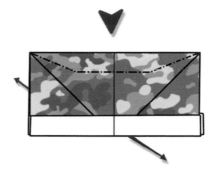

7 Turn your model over, and repeat steps 5 and 6 on the other side.

8 Open the cap slightly, while pushing down gently on the top to shape the cap.

GLOSSARY

cargo (KAHR-goh) The load of goods carried by an airplane, a ship, or an automobile.

instructions (in-STRUK-shunz) Explanations or directions.

military (MIH-luh-ter-ee) Having to do with the part of the government, such as the army or navy, that keeps its citizens safe.

origami (or-uh-GAH-mee) The art of folding paper into decorative shapes or objects.

personnel (per-sun-EL) The people employed in any work, business, or service.

proportions (pruh-POR-shunz) Proper or equal shares.

sculptures (SKULP-cherz) Works of art that have shape to them, such as statues, or carved objects, and may be made of wood, stone, metal, plaster, or even paper.

techniques (tek-NEEKZ) Methods or ways of bringing about a desired result in a science, an art, a sport, or a profession.

tools (TOOLZ) Objects that are specially made to help people do work.

FURTHER READING

Doeden, Matt. *The U.S. Air Force*. Pebble Plus: Military Branches. Mankato, MN: Capstone Press, 2008.

Jackson, Kay. *Military Helicopters in Action*. Amazing Military Vehicles. New York: PowerKids Press, 2009.

Wood, Alix. *Serving in the Air Force*. Protecting Our Country. New York: PowerKids Press, 2013.

WEBSITES

Due to the changing nature of Internet links, PowerKids Press has developed an online list of websites related to the subject of this book. This site is updated regularly. Please use this link to access the list:
www.powerkids.com/orar/air/

INDEX